The Odyssey of the Soul

O SON OF MAN! Thou art My dominion and My dominion perisheth not, wherefore fearest thou thy perishing? Thou art My light and My light shall never be extinguished, why dost thou dread extinction? Thou art my glory and My glory fadeth not; thou art My robe and My robe shall never be outworn. Abide then in thy love for Me, that thou mayest find Me in the realm of glory.[1]

Bahá'u'lláh

The Odyssey of the Soul

by

Artemus Lamb

GEORGE RONALD
OXFORD

GEORGE RONALD, Publisher
46 High Street, Kidlington, Oxford OX5 2DN

© ARTEMUS LAMB 1995
All Rights Reserved
Reprinted 2003

British Library Cataloguing in Publication Data
A catalogue record for this book is available
from the British Library

ISBN 0-85398-401-8

Cover illustration *Other Words* by Marcia Coburn

Typeset by Leith Editorial Services, Abingdon, Oxon, UK

Printed in Great Britain by
Cromwell Press Ltd, Trowbridge, Wilts BA14 0XB

Contents

Prologue   1

The First Stage   3

     The Birth of the Soul   5

The Second Stage   7

     Birth into this World   9
     The Destiny of the Human Being   10
     Fulfilling a High Destiny   12
     The Manifestations of God   16
     The Riches of the Next World   19
     The Symbolism of the Holy Books   21
     Detachment from this World   23
     Hardships and Tests   26
     Prayer   30
     Meditation   33
     The Maturity of Humanity   37
     The True Religion of God   39
     The End of the Second Stage   41

The Third Stage   45

     A World Completely Different   47
     Progress of the Soul in the Next World   52
     Dreams: Proofs of Immortality   56
     End of the Odyssey   60

Epilogue   65
   The Supreme Goal   67
   Divine Justice   70

Bibliography   74

References   76

Prologue

SURELY you have had the experience of travelling in a car or bus and, in a meditative mood, speculated on what lay ahead. All is peaceful. The only sound is the lulling rhythmic throb of the motor. You feel isolated from the problems and agitation of daily life.

What lies ahead? You can only see for a short distance, for a curve, a hill or perhaps other vehicles obstruct the view. What kind of scenery will you pass? Will some trouble occur, a flat tyre, engine trouble, perhaps even an accident? What will the final destination be like and when will you arrive?

Our life in the ephemeral world is very similar. Where are we going? When will we arrive at our destination and what will it be like? What experiences will happen to us on the way? What possible perils will we encounter on our road and what can we do to avoid them or, at least, soften them? What preparations can we make for our journey?

The writings of the Bahá'í Faith help answer these questions.

The First Stage

The Birth of the Soul

MAN – the true man – is soul, not body; though physically man belongs to the animal kingdom, yet his soul lifts him above the rest of creation.[2]

'Abdu'l-Bahá

The soul is not a combination of elements, it is not composed of many atoms, it is of one indivisible substance and therefore eternal. It is entirely out of the order of the physical creation; it is immortal![3]

'Abdu'l-Bahá

The soul of man is the sun by which his body is illumined, and from which it draweth its sustenance . . .[4]

Bahá'u'lláh

The soul begins its odyssey at the moment of conception. The traveller cannot make any preparation for this stage of the journey. The traveller's individuality, race, sex, nationality, location, date of conception, intelligence and capacities are all determined according to the will of God.

The traveller begins its life in an embryo which passes through different forms, the earliest ones very basic and quite unattractive, until it reaches the form of the human being. These forms represent the different ages that the human species has traversed in its long evolution. Throughout each stage the human, while perhaps looking like some other creature, has been a human being. So it is in this first stage of the odyssey of the soul: the embryo in which it finds itself passes through many stages, but it is always a human being.

During this first stage the soul receives, without any effort on its part, the material body with which it will be associated during the second stage of its journey. The physical and mental faculties and powers, including the five senses, are endowed upon it, for these it will need in the second stage of its odyssey.

The Second Stage

Birth into this World

THE SECOND STAGE of the soul's odyssey commences with the birth of the baby into this world. Suddenly the soul finds itself in a world infinitely larger and lighter than the confined and dark world of the womb, a world in which the physical and intellectual powers received in the matrix world will begin to function.

Now the traveller possesses, within certain limits, free will, that is, the power to choose his road. Which road to choose? The straight and spiritual road leading to God or the tortuous and dark materialistic road leading to the fleeting and ephemeral things of this world? This decision is, without doubt, the most serious and of the most consequence of any to be made in life for it will determine the entire course and final destiny of the traveller.

The Destiny of the Human Being

THE BIBLE tells us that God created humans in His image and likeness. This refers not to the physical body but rather to that inner reality of every human being, regardless of its race, sex, nationality or social position, that is potentially capable of reflecting the attributes of its Creator.

Bahá'u'lláh emphatically confirms this, repeatedly emphasizing the blessings and high station that the Creator has conferred on His creation and passionately exhorting us to rise to attain them:

> How lofty is the station which man, if he but choose to fulfil his high destiny, can attain! To what depths of degradation he can sink, depths which the meanest of creatures have never reached![5]

> The Purpose of the one true God, exalted be His glory, in revealing Himself unto men is to lay bare those gems that lie hidden within the mine of their true and inmost selves.[6]

> Man is the supreme Talisman. Lack of a proper education hath, however, deprived him of that which he doth inherently possess . . . Regard man as a mine rich in gems of inestimable value. Education can, alone, cause it to reveal its treasures, and enable mankind to benefit therefrom.[7]

Speaking as God's mouthpiece Bahá'u'lláh says:

> O Son of Man! Upon the tree of effulgent glory I have hung for thee the choicest fruits, wherefore hast thou turned away and contented thyself with that which is less good? Return then unto that which is better for thee in the realm on high.[8]

> O Son of Spirit! Noble have I created thee, yet thou hast abased thyself. Rise then unto that for which thou wast created.[9]

> O Son of the Supreme! To the eternal I call thee, yet thou dost seek that which perisheth. What hath made thee turn away from Our desire and seek thine own?[10]

Thus the soul is destined to achieve a noble station, yet, unfortunately, too often turns away from that which will enable it to fulfil its destiny with ease.

Fulfilling a High Destiny

'THE PURPOSE OF GOD in creating man', declared Bahá'u'lláh, 'hath been, and will ever be, to enable him to know his Creator and to attain His Presence.'[11] Yet the sacred books of all the world religions confirm that God is invisible, unknowable, inscrutable, hidden in His own world. How can the soul come to know its Creator and attain His presence when Bahá'u'lláh Himself states:

> All that the sages and mystics have said or written have never exceeded, nor can they ever hope to exceed, the limitations to which man's finite mind hath been strictly subjected . . . Whoever pondereth this truth in his heart will readily admit that there are certain limits which no human being can possibly transgress. Every attempt which, from the beginning that hath no beginning, hath been made to visualize and know God is limited by the exigencies of His own creation – a creation which He, through the operation of His own Will and for the purposes of none other but His own Self, hath called into being.[12]

And again:

> To every discerning and illuminated heart it is evident that God, the unknowable Essence, the Divine Being,

is immensely exalted beyond every human attribute, such as corporeal existence, ascent and descent, egress and regress. Far be it from His glory that human tongue should adequately recount His praise, or that human heart comprehend His fathomless mystery. He is, and hath ever been, veiled in the ancient eternity of His Essence, and will remain in His Reality everlastingly hidden from the sight of men.[13]

The soul comes to learn of its Creator through Prophets, Messengers, Manifestations who are chosen by God to act as intermediaries between the Supreme Being and His Creation and who are the perfect mirrors of His attributes.

As a token of His mercy . . . and as a proof of His loving-kindness, He hath manifested unto men the Day Stars of His divine guidance, the Symbols of His divine unity, and hath ordained the knowledge of these sanctified Beings to be identical with the knowledge of His own Self.[14]

When the traveller 'comes into the presence' of the Manifestation of God, that is, when it learns of and accepts the teaching of the Manifestation, it has attained the presence of God Himself:

Whoso recognizeth them hath recognized God. Whoso hearkeneth to their call, hath hearkened to the Voice of God, and whoso testifieth to the truth of their Revelation, hath testified to the truth of God Himself. Whoso turneth away from them, hath turned away from God, and whoso disbelieveth in them, hath disbelieved in God. Every one of them is the Way of God that connecteth this world with the realms above, and

the Standard of His Truth unto every one in the kingdoms of earth and heaven. They are the Manifestations
of God amidst men, the evidences of His Truth, and
the signs of His glory.[15]

The soul is endowed not only with the destiny of
coming to know God but with the capacity to do so:

> Having created the world and all that liveth and
> moveth therein, He, through the direct operation of
> His unconstrained and sovereign Will, chose to confer
> upon man the unique distinction and capacity to know
> Him and to love Him – a capacity that must needs be
> regarded as the generating impulse and the primary
> purpose underlying the whole of creation . . . Upon the
> inmost reality of each and every created thing He hath
> shed the light of one of His names, and made it a
> recipient of the glory of one of His attributes. Upon
> the reality of man, however, He hath focused the radi-
> ance of all of His names and attributes, and made it a
> mirror of His own Self. Alone of all created things
> man hath been singled out for so great a favour, so
> enduring a bounty.[16]

However, the ability of the soul to come to know its
Creator is sleeping and needs to be awakened:

> These energies with which the Day Star of Divine
> bounty and Source of heavenly guidance hath
> endowed the reality of man lie, however, latent within
> him, even as the flame is hidden within the candle and
> the rays of light are potentially present in the lamp.
> The radiance of these energies may be obscured by
> worldly desires even as the light of the sun can be con-
> cealed beneath the dust and dross which cover the
> mirror. Neither the candle nor the lamp can be lighted

through their own unaided efforts, nor can it ever be possible for the mirror to free itself from its dross. It is clear and evident that until a fire is kindled the lamp will never be ignited, and unless the dross is blotted out from the face of the mirror it can never represent the image of the sun nor reflect its light and glory.[17]

The power to light the fire within the soul, to arouse the sleeping potential of the soul to recognize and love its Creator, is the Holy Spirit, brought by the Manifestation of God.

The power of the Spirit manifests itself in this world in different degrees or 'kingdoms'.[18] For example, in the mineral kingdom this power is manifested as cohesion, in the vegetable kingdom as growth, in the animal kingdom as the ability to sense the physical world and in the human kingdom as the ability to reason. Beyond these are the Spirit of Faith and the Holy or Most Great Spirit.

While every person is born with the human spirit, which confers the faculties of the intellect as well as the powers of the lower kingdoms, one does not really 'live' until the Spirit of Faith is obtained through the sincere recognition and acceptance of the Manifestation of God for the epoch in which one lives and the application of His laws and teachings in one's daily life. This is the primary and supreme goal of every soul while on its odyssey in this world. Until this step is taken, the soul will not be able to fulfil its ultimate destiny.

The Manifestations of God

THAT THE SOUL can recognize the Manifestation of God for the age into which it is born is due to the nature of the appearance of the Manifestations. There is, in reality, only one religion, the religion of God. This is revealed progressively by a series or chain of Manifestations. From time immemorial the Manifestations have come into the world at intervals, often hundreds of years apart, and will continue to do so until the end that has no end.

The revelation of each Manifestation is imparted in accordance with the requirements and capacities of the age and has two main aspects: a repetition of the basic, eternal truths and social laws and teachings which differ in each age according to the evolving needs and possibilities of the time. Among the Manifestations recorded by history are Krishna, Moses, Zoroaster, Buddha, Christ, Muḥammad and Bahá'u'lláh.

These great Manifestations, as well as revealing new divine teachings and laws and bringing the power and guidance of the Holy Spirit, act as pure and perfect mirrors of the light, power, love and other attributes of the Creator. We can think of this in terms of the physical sun. If a mirror is placed so that the sun is reflected in it, the disk of the sun will be seen in the mirror. An ignorant person might even think that the sun had come down and entered the mirror, while the truth is that the sun has stayed in the sky. The Manifestations of God are like these mirrors, reflecting perfectly the light, power and other attributes of God. God does not come down and dwell within them.

All the great religions of the world have prophecies of a day when a universal Manifestation of God will appear, one who will unite humankind and establish a reign of justice and peace upon the earth. This transcendent event is known as the Day of the Lord, the Day of God, the Great Announcement. The Bahá'í Faith proclaims that Bahá'u'lláh is that great universal Manifestation:

> To Israel He was neither more nor less than the incarnation of the 'Everlasting Father', the 'Lord of Hosts' come down 'with ten thousands of saints'; to Christendom Christ returned 'in the glory of the Father', to Shí'ah Islám the return of the Imám Husayn; to Sunní Islám the descent of the 'Spirit of God' (Jesus Christ); to the Zoroastrians the promised Sháh-Bahrám; to the Hindus the reincarnation of Krishna; to the Buddhists the fifth Buddha.[19]

Bahá'u'lláh Himself declared:

> The time foreordained unto the peoples and kindreds of the earth is now come. The promises of God, as recorded in the holy Scriptures, have all been fulfilled. Out of Zion hath gone forth the Law of God, and Jerusalem, and the hills and land thereof, are filled with the glory of His Revelation. Happy is the man

that pondereth in his heart that which hath been revealed in the Books of God, the Help in Peril, the Self-Subsisting.[20]

The soul on its journey through this life needs to ponder on its own response to such a claim.

The Riches of the Next World

J N THE FIRST STAGE of its odyssey the wayfarer is given all the faculties and powers it will need in the second stage of its journey. In the second stage, however, it is the soul itself which must acquire those qualities needed for the third stage of its travels. This is the key point: *the spiritual faculties are not bestowed gratuitously; they must be earned through the soul's own efforts and actions in this world.*

This is a serious matter, as Muḥammad has said, for without the spiritual qualities of love, compassion, faith, humility, selflessness, justice, sanctity, purity of heart, truthfulness, integrity and so on, it will not be possible for the soul to function adequately in or to enjoy the bounties of the third stage of its odyssey. It would be, as 'Abdu'l-Bahá so graphically puts it, as though the soul were 'dead, blind, deaf and dumb'.[21]

This condition of spiritual poverty is the true inferno. The terms 'heaven' or 'paradise', 'hell' and 'inferno' do not refer to places but to spiritual conditions. Simply stated, heaven or paradise is a spiritual state of nearness to God, while inferno or hell is spiritual separation from God. In the *Book of Certitude* Bahá'u'lláh affirms:

In every age and century, the purpose of the Prophets of God and their chosen ones hath been no other but to affirm the spiritual significance of the terms 'life', 'resurrection', and 'judgement'. If one will ponder but for a while this utterance of 'Alí in his heart, one will surely discover all mysteries hidden in the terms 'grave', 'tomb', 'sirat', 'paradise' and 'hell'.[22]

Reflect for a moment upon the state of a soul which has made no preparation for the coming world. Take, for example, the case of a person wealthy in all the material aspects of life on earth – money, material possessions, high social position, business prestige, political powers, worldly fame – but who has never had any real spiritual training or, perhaps, given any thought to spiritual or religious matters. Suddenly he finds himself in a world where only the spiritual attributes have any importance and value. This is a true inferno for that soul.

The Symbolism of the Holy Books

ONE OF THE TESTS facing the soul on its odyssey is how to understand the teachings of the Manifestation of God as they appear in the holy books. The question of interpretation is of vital importance, as it is the source of some of the greatest divisions of the religions and often creates rivalry and even open hostility among those who take one or other view point. One side believes in a literal interpretation of the holy books, while the other believes that these books are to be understood symbolically.

Bahá'u'lláh states that both positions are correct:

It is evident unto thee that the Birds of Heaven and Doves of Eternity speak a twofold language. One language, the outward language, is devoid of allusions, is unconcealed and unveiled; that it may be a guiding lamp and a beaconing light whereby wayfarers may attain the heights of holiness, and seekers may advance into the realm of eternal reunion. Such are the unveiled traditions and the evident verses already mentioned. The other language is veiled and concealed, so that whatever lieth hidden in the heart of the malevolent may be made manifest and their innermost being be disclosed. Thus hath Ṣádiq, son of Muḥammad, spoken: 'God verily will test them and sift them.' This is the divine standard, this is the Touchstone of God, wherewith He proveth His servants.[23]

Thus the wayfarer must study the books of God and discern those verses that are intended to be understood literally and those that are symbolic.

Detachment from this World

ALL THE MANIFESTATIONS OF GOD have emphasized the need for the soul, while it is in this world, to be detached from it. Bahá'u'lláh describes the world as a mere illusion:

> The world is but a show, vain and empty, a mere nothing, bearing the semblance of reality. Set not your affections upon it. Break not the bond that uniteth you with your Creator, and be not of those that have erred and strayed from His ways. Verily I say, the world is like the vapour in a desert, which the thirsty dreameth to be water and striveth after it with all his might, until when he cometh unto it, he findeth it to be mere illusion. It may, moreover, be likened unto the lifeless image of the beloved whom the lover hath sought and found, in the end, after long search and to his utmost regret, to be such as cannot 'fatten nor appease his hunger'.[24]

'Know ye', Bahá'u'lláh explains, 'that by "the world" is meant your unawareness of Him Who is your Maker, and your absorption in aught else but Him . . . Whatsoever deterreth you, in this Day, from loving God is nothing but the world. Flee it, that ye may be numbered with the blest.' Then He adds:

> Should a man wish to adorn himself with the ornaments of the earth, to wear its apparels, or partake of

23

the benefits it can bestow, no harm can befall him, if he alloweth nothing whatever to intervene between him and God, for God hath ordained every good thing, whether created in the heavens or in the earth, for such of His servants as truly believe in Him. Eat ye, O people, of the good things which God hath allowed you, and deprive not yourselves from His wondrous bounties. Render thanks and praise unto Him, and be of them that are truly thankful.[25]

A life of asceticism and seclusion is not required of the soul on its odyssey through this world. Even those who would spend their lives in prayer and devotion are encouraged not to live in seclusion:

The pious deeds of the monks and priests among the followers of the Spirit [Christ] – upon Him be the peace of God – are remembered in His presence. In this Day, however, let them give up the life of seclusion and direct their steps towards the open world and busy themselves with that which will profit themselves and others.[26]

O people of the earth! Living in seclusion or practising asceticism is not acceptable in the presence of God. It behoveth them that are endued with insight and understanding to observe that which will cause joy and radiance . . . Deprive not yourselves of the bounties which have been created for your sake.[27]

It is enjoined upon every one of you to engage in some form of occupation, such as crafts, trades and the like. We have graciously exalted your engagement in such work to the rank of worship unto God, the True One . . . Occupy yourselves with that which profiteth yourselves and others . . . The most despised of men in the sight of God are those who sit idly and beg.[28]

In short, detachment does not mean physical separation from the world. The soul is to enter into the life of this world and, in intimate contact with other members of the human family, build an ever-advancing civilization, yet placing first in its life its Creator and remembering the high destiny awaiting it. If the material things and pleasures of this passing world become of primary importance, and the soul becomes attached to them, it is a signal that the wayfarer is on the wrong road and is in danger. To live in this world and yet be detached from it requires deep spiritual understanding and maturity and constant vigilance. As Bahá'u'lláh points out so vividly, 'Rejoice not in the things ye possess; tonight they are yours, tomorrow others will possess them.'[29]

Hardships and Tests

WHILE ON ITS ODYSSEY the soul will encounter many hardships and be faced with many tests. 'Abdu'l-Bahá was once asked whether the soul progresses more through suffering or joy. He replied:

> The mind and spirit of man advance when he is tried by suffering. The more the ground is ploughed the better the seed will grow, the better the harvest will be. Just as the plough furrows the earth deeply, purifying it of weeds and thistles, so suffering and tribulation free man from the petty affairs of this worldly life until he arrives at a state of complete detachment. His attitude in this world will be that of divine happiness. Man is, so to speak, unripe: the heat of the fire of suffering will mature him. Look back to the times past and you will find that the greatest men have suffered most.[30]

The reality is that this world is not the soul's home but only, as 'Abdu'l-Bahá says, its first classroom, that is, a place of education, training and preparation for the more advanced life of the third stage of the soul's odyssey. Therefore, the traveller must, in passing through this world, experience a certain number of difficulties and tests, otherwise the soul will not be properly prepared. When the soul understands this, it has won the first battle, as it were, for now it will accept tests, not with rebellion and complaints, but as stepping stones in its spiritual growth and maturation, as part of the odyssey itself. As Shoghi Effendi asks, 'Has not Bahá'u'lláh assured us that sufferings and privations are blessings in disguise, that through them our inner spiritual forces become stimulated, purified and ennobled?'[31]

> We should not, however, forget that an essential characteristic of this world is hardship and tribulation and that it is by overcoming them that we achieve our moral and spiritual development. As the Master says, sorrow is like furrows, the deeper they go the more plentiful are the fruits we obtain.[32]

> . . . as we suffer these misfortunes we must remember that the Prophets of God Themselves were not immune from these things which men suffer. They knew sorrow, illness and pain too. They rose above these things through Their spirits, and that is what we must try and do too, when afflicted. The troubles of this world pass, and what we have left is what we have made of our souls; so it is to this we must look – to becoming more spiritual, drawing nearer to God, no matter what our human minds and bodies go through.[33]

As 'Abdu'l-Bahá explained:

> Tests are benefits from God, for which we should thank Him. Grief and sorrow do not come to us by chance, they are sent to us by the Divine Mercy for our own perfecting . . . Men who suffer not, attain no perfection. The plant most pruned by the gardeners is that one which, when the summer comes, will have the most beautiful blossoms and the most abundant fruit.[34]

> To attain eternal happiness one must suffer. He who
> has reached the state of self-sacrifice has true joy.
> Temporal joy will vanish.[35]

In summary, the Creator, in His perfect and deep love
for us, sends to each of us, at intervals, difficulties
and tests to help the soul develop and mature and to
become purified and fortified. All is for the welfare
of the soul, for its progress and true happiness. Only
the Creator knows what is best for the soul. If the soul
places itself under the guidance and protection of the
Manifestation of God for the epoch in which it finds
itself – in this age, Bahá'u'lláh – and tries sincerely
to live in accordance with the teachings and laws
revealed by Him, it will attain an unimaginable and
eternal happiness, immensely greater than any trivial
and temporary pleasure derived from the ephemeral
things of this world.

On the other hand, there are difficulties and tribula-
tions that come to the soul through its own misdoings
and transgressions. These are punishments but are
also blessings in disguise, for they show the soul, in
a tangible way, that such actions only bring trouble
and unhappiness.

The wise person does not seek out tests or fabricate
them, but rather waits with faith and valour for those
that the Almighty sends.

This theme, so carefully explained in the Bahá'í
teachings, is of the utmost importance, particularly in
these troublesome and chaotic times through which
humanity is passing.

> Were it not for tests, pure gold could not be distin-
> guished from the impure. Were it not for tests, the

courageous could not be separated from the cowardly. Were it not for tests, the people of faithfulness could not be known from the disloyal . . . Were it not for tests, sparkling gems could not be known from worthless pebbles.[36]

O Son of Man! My calamity is My providence, outwardly it is fire and vengeance, but inwardly it is light and mercy. Hasten thereunto that thou mayest become an eternal light and an immortal spirit. This is My command unto thee, do thou observe it.[37]

Prayer

Among the essential preparations that the wayfarer should make for his sure passage in this world as well as for his life in the third stage of his odyssey are prayer and meditation.

Bahá'u'lláh declared that 'in all Dispensations the law of prayer hath constituted a fundamental element of the Revelation of all the Prophets of God'.[38] Just as the human body requires daily material nourishment in order to be strong and healthy, the soul likewise needs daily the spiritual sustenance of prayer. As Bahá'u'lláh asserts: 'O Son of Being! Love Me, that I may love thee. If thou lovest Me not, My love can in no wise reach thee. Know this, O servant.'[39]

The love of God always surrounds the soul but, in accordance with this spiritual law, unless the soul turns towards its Creator, His love will not reach it. This is like the radio, which must conform to physical laws: if we do not turn the radio on, it cannot receive the signal, even though the signal is always there. As 'Abdu'l-Bahá explains:

> . . . man must seek capacity and develop readiness. As long as he lacks susceptibility to divine influences, he is incapable of reflecting the light and assimilating its benefits. Sterile soil will produce nothing, even if the

cloud of mercy pours rain upon it a thousand years. . .
No matter how beautiful the melody, the ear that is
deaf cannot hear it, cannot receive the call of the
Supreme Concourse . . . Therefore, we must ever
strive for capacity and seek readiness.[40]

When the vessel is enlarged the water increases, and
when the thirst grows the bounty of the cloud becomes
agreeable to the taste of man. This is the mystery of
supplication and the wisdom of stating one's wants.[41]

'We must live in the state of prayer,' 'Abdu'l-Bahá
states.

Prayer is conversation with God, the most blessed
condition is the state of prayer. It creates wakefulness
and celestial sentiments. Prayer and supplication are
so effective that they inspire the heart for the whole
day with ideals and supreme sanctity and tranquillity.[42]

He also promises that prayer is a means of avoiding
unnecessary tests.

At the same time, prayers that are automatic and for-
mal, that do not touch the core of the heart, are of no
avail. The efficacy of prayer depends upon freedom
of the heart from extraneous suggestions and mun-
dane thoughts. 'The worshipper must pray with a
detached spirit, unconditional surrender of the will,
concentrated attention, and a magnetic spiritual pas-
sion.'[43]

That is to say, prayers recited mechanically merely
as a duty, or simply to comply with a ritual or when
in a hurry do not have much effect. In the words of
the Báb:

The most acceptable prayer is the one offered with the utmost spirituality and radiance; its prolongation hath not been and is not beloved by God. The more detached and the purer the prayer, the more acceptable is it in the presence of God.[44]

At the same time it must be remembered that Bahá'u'lláh has said that the very recitation of the words of God can have an influence on the soul:

Whoso reciteth, in the privacy of his chamber, the verses revealed by God, the scattering angels of the Almighty shall scatter abroad the fragrance of the words uttered by his mouth, and shall cause the heart of every righteous man to throb. Though he may, at first, remain unaware of its effect, yet the virtue of the grace vouchsafed unto him must needs sooner or later exercise its influence upon his soul.[45]

As this verse indicates, the prayers of the Divine Manifestations possess special power. The beautiful prayers of Bahá'u'lláh, the Báb and 'Abdu'l-Bahá deeply affect the soul and are indispensable for its odyssey.

Meditation

BAHÁ'U'LLÁH reaffirmed the saying that 'One hour's reflection is preferable to seventy years of pious worship'.[46]

In this age of the maturity or coming of age of humanity, blind faith is no longer sufficient for the progress of the soul. Now 'conscious knowledge',[47] as 'Abdu'l-Bahá described it, is required. The mature person wishes to understand the will of God and religious and spiritual matters as much as possible, and should do so. This requires study and reflection on the realities of life and on the teachings of God as revealed by His Manifestations in order to seek out their meaning. Meditation is an indispensable method of doing so.

Meditation is not the assumption of certain postures or the uttering of certain words or the practice of certain disciplines. The soul is free to search out the method of meditation that seems best for it but 'should guard against superstitious or foolish ideas creeping into it'.[48]

'Abdu'l-Bahá spoke of meditation while in Paris:

> Bahá'u'lláh says there is a sign (from God) in every phenomenon: the sign of the intellect is contemplation and the sign of contemplation is silence . . .[49]

'Abdu'l-Bahá further explained:

> Meditation is the key for opening the doors of mysteries. In that state man abstracts himself: in that state man withdraws himself from all outside objects; in that subjective mood he is immersed in the ocean of spiritual life and can unfold the secrets of things-in-themselves. To illustrate this, think of man as endowed with two kinds of sight; when the power of insight is being used the outward power of vision does not see.
>
> This faculty of meditation frees man from the animal nature, discerns the reality of things, puts man in touch with God.[50]

> The spirit of man is itself informed and strengthened during meditation; through it affairs of which man knew nothing are unfolded before his view.[51]

> Through the faculty of meditation man attains to eternal life; through it he receives the breath of the Holy Spirit – the bestowal of the Spirit is given in reflection and meditation.[52]

> You cannot apply the name 'man' to any being void of this faculty of meditation; without it he would be a mere animal, lower than the beasts.[53]

Thus, by 'contemplation', 'reflection' or 'meditation' is meant that the soul reflects deeply and with complete concentration and detachment from all else. Certainly, on beginning to meditate, it is of tremendous help if the soul asks for divine guidance and protection.

The soul may meditate on material or spiritual matters for, as 'Abdu'l-Bahá explained:

The meditative faculty is akin to the mirror; if you put it before earthly objects it will reflect them. Therefore if the spirit of man is contemplating earthly subjects he will be informed of these.

But if you turn the mirror of your spirits heavenwards, the heavenly constellations and the rays of the Sun of Reality will be reflected in your hearts, and the virtues of the Kingdom will be obtained.[54]

It is through meditation that the sciences, arts, the great inventions and discoveries have been made and developed.

One of the fundamental teachings of Bahá'u'lláh is the responsibility and right of the soul to investigate truth independently. Bahá'u'lláh asserts that as a fundamental fact of creation every human soul inherently possesses the power to search out the truth and discover it and that, further, it is the responsibility of the soul to do so. In the past, it was the custom for most people to rely on the judgement of others, especially in religious matters, but today this responsibility is given to the individual soul. Of course, one may consult with others; indeed, Bahá'u'lláh recommends consultation in all matters, but the soul must make its own decision at the last. In the majestic words of Bahá'u'lláh:

O Son of Spirit! The best beloved of all things in My sight is Justice; turn not away therefrom if thou desirest Me, and neglect it not that I may confide in thee. By its aid thou shalt see with thine own eyes and not through the eyes of others, and shalt know of thine own knowledge and not through the knowledge of thy neighbour.[55]

Only when the lamp of search, of earnest striving, of longing desire, of passionate devotion, of fervid love, of rapture, and ecstasy, is kindled within the seeker's heart, and the breeze of His loving-kindness is wafted upon his soul, will the darkness of error be dispelled, the mists of doubts and misgivings be dissipated, and the lights of knowledge and certitude envelop his being. At that hour will the mystic Herald, bearing the joyful tidings of the Spirit, shine forth from the City of God resplendent as the morn, and, through the trumpet-blast of knowledge, will awaken the heart, the soul, and the spirit from the slumber of negligence. Then will the manifold favours and outpouring grace of the holy and everlasting Spirit confer such new life upon the seeker that he will find himself endowed with a new eye, a new ear, a new heart, and a new mind. He will contemplate the manifest signs of the universe, and will penetrate the hidden mysteries of the soul. Gazing with the eye of God, he will perceive within every atom a door that leadeth him to the stations of absolute certitude. He will discover in all things the mysteries of divine Revelation and the evidences of an everlasting manifestation.

I swear by God! Were he that treadeth the path of guidance and seeketh to scale the heights of righteousness to attain unto this glorious and supreme station, he would inhale at a distance of a thousand leagues the fragrance of God, and would perceive the resplendent morn of a divine Guidance rising above the dayspring of all things. Each and every thing, however small, would be to him a revelation, leading him to his Beloved, the Object of his quest.[56]

The Maturity of Humanity

EVERYONE KNOWS that a human being develops by stages – infancy, childhood, adolescence, adulthood – and that in each stage the individual receives new powers and concepts and acquires new habits and styles of living. The Bahá'í teachings emphasize that humanity, like the individual human being, is a single organism and also passes through these same stages. Humanity is now entering its maturity. In the words of 'Abdu'l-Bahá:

> Similarly there are periods and stages in the collective life of humanity. At one time it was passing through its stage of childhood, at another its period of youth, but now it has entered its long-predicted phase of maturity, the evidences of which are everywhere apparent . . . That which was applicable to human needs during the early history of the race can neither meet nor satisfy the demands of this day, this period of newness and consummation. Humanity has emerged from its former state of limitation and preliminary training. Man must now become imbued with new virtues and powers, new moral standards, new capacities. New bounties, perfect bestowals, are awaiting and already descending upon him. The gifts and blessings of the period of youth, although timely and sufficient during the adolescence of mankind, are now incapable of meeting the requirements of its maturity.[57]

What practical importance does this have for the soul on its odyssey? For one thing, it means that 'new virtues and powers, new moral standards, new capacities' are now required to meet the needs and possibilities of the new stage of maturity. Further, a completely new and different style of life needs to be developed, with new and more mature concepts guiding it, and different ways of thinking and acting. Indeed, in Shoghi Effendi's words, a 'new race of men' needs to come into being.[58] And since each soul is a part of humanity, a complete change in the life of every soul is required. The toys of the soul's childhood no longer have any use or hold any interest.

From where will come the inspiration, the guidance and the spiritual force for this new life? The religions of past ages were revealed to meet the needs of the preliminary stages of humankind's evolution. Thus it is from the revelation of Bahá'u'lláh, which was sent by the Creator for exactly this purpose, that such guidance will come.

The True Religion of God

TRUE RELIGION is not something practised only on certain days of the week or at certain hours of the day and only in those circumstances when it seems convenient. Rather, religion should be the heart and base of both the inner and outer aspects of the soul's entire life at all times, throughout its odyssey.

Often when one thinks of religion there come to mind such images as altars, priests, hymns, sermons, creeds, rituals and ceremonies. All of these are, in reality, the outer expression of religion, not its essence; its adornments, not its reality. The true religion of God has always consisted of the pure guidance, teachings, laws and ordinances revealed from epoch to epoch by the Manifestations of God and of the inspiration of these beings and their lives. As 'Abdu'l-Bahá expressed it:

> The cornerstone of the religion of God is the acquisition of the divine perfections and the sharing in His manifold bestowals. The essential purpose of faith and belief is to ennoble the inner being of man with the outpourings of grace from on high. If this be not attained, it is, indeed, deprivation itself.[59]

> If he comes under the shadow of the True Educator and is rightly trained, he becomes the essence of

essences, the light of lights, the spirit of spirits; he becomes the centre of the divine appearances, the source of spiritual qualities, the rising-place of heavenly lights, and the receptacle of divine inspirations.[60]

In this day of the coming of age of humanity, the mature soul must study, understand, practise, teach and administer its religion.

The End of the Second Stage

EVENTUALLY comes the time for the wayfarer, whether prepared or not, to leave his temporary home in the physical world and continue his eternal odyssey. Simply, the connection between the physical body and the soul is severed. The body, which has served as the vehicle of the soul by which it has journeyed through the physical world, is no longer needed for the third stage of the soul's odyssey and remains on earth. It gradually decomposes into dust, its atoms are dispersed and it is eventually assimilated by the different kingdoms of creation. The soul, the 'real' person, passes over to the non-material world to continue its odyssey through the endless worlds of God.

The soul enters the next world in the same condition in which it left this one. According to all the great religions, it will be 'judged' on arrival for its life and acts on earth. Bahá'u'lláh Himself declared:

> Thou shalt, after thy departure, discover what We have revealed unto thee, and shalt find all thy doings recorded in the Book wherein the works of all them that dwell on earth, be they greater or less than the weight of an atom, are noted down.[61]

It is clear and evident that all men shall, after their physical death, estimate the worth of their deeds, and realize all that their hands have wrought. I swear by the Day Star that shineth above the horizon of Divine power! They that are the followers of the one true God shall, the moment they depart out of this life, experience such joy and gladness as would be impossible to describe, while they that live in error shall be seized with such fear and trembling, and shall be filled with such consternation, as nothing can exceed. Well is it with him that hath quaffed the choice and incorruptible wine of faith through the gracious favour and the manifold bounties of Him Who is the Lord of all Faiths.[62]

In view of this Bahá'u'lláh urges the soul:

Set before thine eyes God's unerring Balance and, as one standing in His Presence, weigh in that Balance thine actions every day, every moment of thy life. Bring thyself to account ere thou art summoned to a reckoning, on the Day when no man shall have strength to stand for fear of God, the Day when the hearts of the heedless ones shall be made to tremble.[63]

And, further:

O Son of Being! Bring thyself to account each day ere thou art summoned to a reckoning; for death, unheralded, shall come upon thee and thou shalt be called to give account for thy deeds.[64]

On the other hand, God, our Creator, in His great love and justice, will not hold the soul responsible for conduct beyond its capacity. As Bahá'u'lláh promises, 'He will never deal unjustly with any one, neither will He task a soul beyond its power.'[65]

A fundamental teaching of Bahá'u'lláh, that helps one greatly to understand things which are otherwise puzzling and aids the soul to be indulgent with other members of the human family, is that all souls have different capacities, that no two are exactly alike:

> Difference of capacity in human individuals is fundamental. It is impossible for all to be alike, all to be equal, all to be wise.[66]

> The whole duty of man in this Day is to attain that share of the flood of grace which God poureth forth for him. Let none, therefore, consider the largeness or smallness of the receptacle. The portion of some might lie in the palm of a man's hand, the portion of others might fill a cup, and of others even a gallon-measure.[67]

What is vitally important is that each soul strives to the utmost to fill, sincerely and faithfully, its vessel. For, as 'Abdu'l-Bahá says, 'From him to whom God has given much in the cradle, God one day will demand much.'[68]

The Third Stage

A World Completely Different

NOW THE TRAVELLER has arrived at his new home. What will it be like? Will he remember his former life? Will he find his dear ones and friends who preceded him? Will he be able to converse with them? What kind of life will he now live?

As far as it is possible to express in the language of this world, the sojourner has not really 'travelled' at all, either when he passed from the world of the matrix into the earthly world or when he moved from that world into the spiritual world; he has only changed condition. The world of the second stage of the soul's odyssey, the earthly world, surrounded the baby in the world of the matrix, and the spiritual world lies about the earthly world. The soul has merely transferred from one state of consciousness, or state of being, to a higher one. As 'Abdu'l-Bahá explained:

> . . . the souls of the children of the Kingdom, after their separation from the body, ascend unto the realm of everlasting life. But if ye ask as to the place, know ye that the world of existence is a single world, although its stations are various and distinct . . . Those souls who are pure and unsullied, upon the dissolution of their elemental frames, hasten away to the world of

God, and that world is within this world. The people
of this world, however, are unaware of that world, and
are even as the mineral and the vegetable that know
nothing of the world of the animal and the world of
man.[69]

Since Bahá'u'lláh brought the teachings and laws of
God for the mature stage of the life of the human
race, He revealed and explained much about the life
of the next world, information not previously
revealed by the Manifestations who preceded Him.
However, He also stated:

> The nature of the soul after death can never be
> described, nor is it meet and permissible to reveal its
> whole character to the eyes of men. The Prophets and
> Messengers of God have been sent down for the sole
> purpose of guiding mankind to the straight Path of
> Truth. The purpose underlying Their revelation hath
> been to educate all men, that they may, at the hour of
> death, ascend, in the utmost purity and sanctity and
> with absolute detachment, to the throne of the Most
> High.[70]

The soul while in this world cannot comprehend the
next, since the 'world beyond is as different from this
world as this world is different from that of the child
while still in the womb of its mother'.[71] How could
the soul understand the third stage of its odyssey,
even if it were fully described? Even our languages,
invented for the second stage of the journey, do not
contain a vocabulary adequate to describe the spiritual world. What we do know of that life, however, is
that it is not the kind of life depicted on the walls and
ceilings of temples and churches, where cherubs and

winged angels rest – how boring and useless would be such a life. Rather, it is the continuation of life in the second stage but on an infinitely higher plane and still with the work of God to be done.

As 'Abdu'l-Bahá states:

> Those who have passed on through death have a sphere of their own. It is not removed from ours; their work, the work of the kingdom, is ours; but it is sanctified from what we call 'time' and 'place'. Time with us is measured by the sun. When there is no more sunrise, and no more sunset, that kind of time does not exist for man. Those who have ascended have different attributes from those who are still on earth, yet there is no real separation.
>
> In prayer there is a mingling of station, a mingling of condition. Pray for them as they pray for you.[72]

'Abdu'l-Bahá further describes this third stage of the journey:

> The outer expression used for the Kingdom is heaven; but this is a comparison and similitude, not a reality or fact, for the Kingdom is not a material place; it is sanctified from time and place. It is a spiritual world, a divine world, and the centre of the Sovereignty of God; it is freed from body and that which is corporeal, and it is purified and sanctified from the imaginations of the human world.[73]

Regarding the form or shape the soul takes in the next world, Bahá'u'lláh says:

> When the soul attaineth the Presence of God, it will assume the form that best befitteth its immortality and is worthy of its celestial habitation.[74]

49

While 'Abdu'l-Bahá states:

> . . . in the other world the human reality doth not
> assume a physical form, rather doth it take on a heav-
> enly form, made up of elements of that heavenly
> realm.[75]

In the next life the soul remembers its life in this
world and is united with its loved ones:

> The mysteries of which man is heedless in the earthly
> world, those will he discover in the heavenly world,
> and there he will be informed of the secrets of the
> truth; how much more will he recognize or discover
> persons with whom he has been associated.
> Undoubtedly the holy souls who find a pure eye and
> are favoured with insight will, in the kingdom of
> lights, be acquainted with all mysteries, and will seek
> the bounty of witnessing the reality of every great
> soul. They will even manifestly behold the beauty of
> God in that world. Likewise they will find all the
> friends of God, both those of the former and recent
> times, present in the heavenly assemblage.
>
> . . . And know thou for a certainty that in the divine
> worlds the spiritual beloved ones will recognize one
> another, and will seek union with each other, but a
> spiritual union. Likewise a love that one may have
> entertained for anyone will not be forgotten in the
> world of the Kingdom, nor wilt thou forget there the
> life thou hadst in the material world.[76]

As Shoghi Effendi explained:

> The possibility of securing union with his beloved in
> the next world is one which the Bahá'í Teachings are
> quite clear about. According to Bahá'u'lláh the soul

retains its individuality and consciousness after death, and is able to commune with other souls. This communion, however, is purely spiritual in character, and is conditioned upon the disinterested and selfless love of the individuals for each other.[77]

And in the words of Bahá'u'lláh Himself:

The honour with which the Hand of Mercy will invest the soul is such as no tongue can adequately reveal, nor any other earthly agency describe. Blessed is the soul which, at the hour of its separation from the body, is sanctified from the vain imaginings of the peoples of the world. Such a soul liveth and moveth in accordance with the Will of its Creator, and entereth the all-highest Paradise. The Maids of Heaven, inmates of the loftiest mansions, will circle around it, and the Prophets of God and His chosen ones will seek its companionship. With them that soul will freely converse, and will recount unto them that which it hath been made to endure in the path of God, the Lord of all worlds. If any man be told that which hath been ordained for such a soul in the worlds of God, the Lord of the throne on high and of earth below, his whole being will instantly blaze out in his great longing to attain that most exalted, that sanctified and resplendent station.[78]

And further:

Know thou that the souls of the people of Bahá, who have entered and been established within the Crimson Ark, shall associate and commune intimately one with another, and shall be so closely associated in their lives, their aspirations, their aims and strivings as to be even as one soul.[79]

51

Progress of the Soul in the Next World

BY WHAT MEANS does the soul progress in the next world?

It is important to bear in mind that the soul in the third stage of its odyssey will not enjoy the same degree of free will as it has in the second stage. In the physical world, the traveller can choose at any moment his road, can decide between good and evil and can either turn towards the spiritual or away from it. In the world of the spirit this is not the case. 'Abdu'l-Bahá points out:

> The progress of man's spirit in the divine world, after the severance of its connection with the body of dust, is through the bounty and grace of the Lord alone, or through the intercession and the sincere prayers of other human souls, or through the charities and important good works which are performed in its name.[80]

> . . . as people in this world are in need of God, they will also need Him in the other world. The creatures are always in need, and God is absolutely independent, whether in this world or in the world to come.
> The wealth of the other world is nearness to God. Consequently, it is certain that those who are near the Divine Court are allowed to intercede, and this inter-

cession is approved by God. But intercession in the other world is not like intercession in this world. It is another thing, another reality, which cannot be expressed in words.[81]

The rich in the other world can help the poor, as the rich can help the poor here . . . What is their merchandise, their wealth? In the other world what is help and assistance? It is intercession. Undeveloped souls must gain progress at first through the supplications of the spiritually rich; afterwards they can progress through their own supplications.[82]

Shoghi Effendi explained that the 'gifts and good deeds done in memory of those who have passed on, are most helpful to the development of their souls in the realms beyond'.[83]

On the other hand, 'Abdu'l-Bahá assured us that progress is possible even for the worst wrong-doers:

As the spirit of man after putting off this material form has an everlasting life, certainly any existing being is capable of making progress; therefore, it is permitted to ask for advancement, forgiveness, mercy, beneficence and blessings for a man after his death because existence is capable of progression. That is why in the prayers of Bahá'u'lláh forgiveness and remission of sins are asked for those who have died.[84]

No doubt the soul on arriving in the next world will experience many surprises, particularly with respect to persons it had known in the physical world. For in the spiritual world the true condition of each soul, often hidden in this world by material trappings, will be recognized. As 'Abdu'l-Bahá states, 'The difference and distinction between men will naturally become realized after their departure from this mortal world. But this distinction is not in respect to place, but in respect to the soul and conscience.[85]

It is possible that a soul that held an apparently high and important position in the physical world will be relatively unknown in the spiritual world, while a seemingly humble and unimportant soul in the second stage will occupy a high station in the third. Recall, the only thing of importance and value in the third stage of the soul's odyssey is its spiritual condition.

Sometimes people wonder whether it would be helpful for those in the physical world to try to communicate with those souls who are already in the next world. The other world is 'within' the physical one and 'Abdu'l-Bahá says that 'the world of existence is a single world'[86] and 'Those who have ascended have different attributes from those who are still on earth, yet there is no real separation. In prayer there is a mingling of station, a mingling of condition.'[87] Apart from whether such communication is possible, perhaps these passages from the Bahá'í teachings will help us better to understand this delicate and, at times, controversial subject. 'Abdu'l-Bahá has said:

> To tamper with psychic forces while in this world interferes with the condition of the soul in the world to come. These forces are real, but, normally, are not active on this plane. The child in the womb has its eyes, ears, hands, feet, etc., but they are not in activity. The whole purpose of life in the material world is the coming forth into the world of Reality, where those forces will become active. They belong to that world.[88]

Shoghi Effendi explained:

> What 'Abdu'l-Bahá always pointed out in this matter
> is that these psychic powers were not to be used in this
> world, and that, indeed, it was dangerous to cultivate
> them here. They should be left dormant, and not
> exploited, even when we do so with the sincere belief
> we are helping others. We do not understand their
> nature and have no way of being sure of what is true
> and what is false in such matters.[89]

Dreams: Proofs of Immortality

ONE OF THE most fascinating mysteries of life is the world of dreams. The body is asleep, the eyes and mouth are closed, yet one has experiences as if awake – sees, hears, speaks, feels, thinks, travels. At times one receives guidance and help; at other times that which occurs in the dream is repeated later, when one is awake. Not all dreams, of course, have significance, but are only dreams of the body, owing to cold, fatigue, tension, worry, happiness, excitement, indigestion and so on. But how is it that one has all these sensations and experiences when the physical faculties are not active? The answer to this has important implications for the soul on its odyssey. It is clear that some aspect of the person is always operating, even without the instrumentality of the body. Bahá'u'lláh explains:

> . . . if we ponder each created thing, we shall witness a myriad perfect wisdoms and learn a myriad new and wondrous truths. One of the created phenomena is the dream. Behold how many secrets are deposited therein, how many wisdoms treasured up, how many worlds concealed. Observe, how thou art asleep in a dwelling, and its doors are barred; on a sudden thou findest thyself in a far-off city, which thou enterest without moving thy feet or wearying thy body; with-

out using thine eyes, thou seest; without taxing thine ears, thou hearest; without a tongue, thou speakest. And perchance when ten years are gone, thou wilt witness in the outer world the very things thou hast dreamed tonight.

. . . First, what is this world, where without eye and ear and hand and tongue a man puts all of these to use? Second, how is it that in the outer world thou seest today the effect of a dream, when thou didst vision it in the world of sleep some ten years past? Consider the difference between these two worlds and the mysteries which they conceal, that thou mayest attain to divine confirmations and heavenly discoveries and enter the regions of holiness.

God, the Exalted, hath placed these signs in men, to the end that philosophers may not deny the mysteries of the life beyond nor belittle that which hath been promised them.[90]

'Abdu'l-Bahá also describes the nature of dreams:

In the time of sleep this body is as though dead; it does not see nor hear; it does not feel; it has no consciousness, no perception – that is to say, the powers of man have become inactive, but the spirit lives and subsists. Nay, its penetration is increased, its flight is higher, and its intelligence is greater. To consider that after the death of the body the spirit perishes is like imagining that a bird in a cage will be destroyed if the cage is broken, though the bird has nothing to fear from the destruction of the cage. Our body is like the cage, and the spirit is like the bird. We see that without the cage this bird flies in the world of sleep; therefore, if the cage becomes broken, the bird will continue and exist. Its feelings will be even more powerful, its perceptions greater, and its happiness increased. In truth, from hell it reaches a paradise of delights because for the thankful birds there is no paradise greater than freedom from the cage. That is why with utmost joy and happiness the martyrs hasten to the plain of sacrifice.[91]

And again Bahá'u'lláh explains:

Consider thy state when asleep. Verily, I say, this phenomenon is the most mysterious of the signs of God amongst men, were they to ponder it in their hearts. Behold how the thing which thou hast seen in thy dream is, after a considerable lapse of time, fully realized. Had the world in which thou didst find thyself in thy dream been identical with the world in which thou livest, it would have been necessary for the event occurring in that dream to have transpired in this world at the very moment of its occurrence. Were it so, you yourself would have borne witness unto it. This being not the case, however, it must necessarily follow that the world in which thou livest is different and apart from that which thou hast experienced in thy dream. This latter world hath neither beginning nor end. It would be true if thou wert to contend that this same world is, as decreed by the All-Glorious and Almighty God, within thy proper self and is wrapped up within thee. It would equally be true to maintain that thy spirit, having transcended the limitations of sleep and having stripped itself of all earthly attachment, hath, by the act of God, been made to traverse a realm which lieth hidden in the innermost reality of this world. Verily I say, the creation of God embraceth worlds besides this world, and creatures apart from these creatures. In each of these worlds He hath ordained things which none can search except Himself, the All-Searching, the All-Wise.[92]

The dream is, therefore, a proof to the soul while in the second stage of its odyssey that the third stage exists. This subject merits profound reflection.

End of the Odyssey

THE SOUL now finds itself in its new home. How long will the traveller stay here? What happens next? What spiritual mountains and valleys will it have to traverse? What will be its activities? Who will be its companions?

Bahá'u'lláh declares, 'Know thou of a truth that the worlds of God are countless in their number, and infinite in their range. None can reckon or comprehend them except God, the All-Knowing, the All-Wise. 'Know thou of a truth',[93] He further states,

> that the soul, after its separation from the body, will continue to progress until it attaineth the presence of God, in a state and condition which neither the revolution of ages and centuries, nor the changes and chances of this world, can alter. It will endure as long as the Kingdom of God, His sovereignty, His dominion and power will endure.[94]

As Shoghi Effendi states:

> Concerning the future life what Bahá'u'lláh says is that the soul will continue to ascend through many worlds. What those worlds are and what their nature is we cannot know. The same way the child in the matrix cannot know this world so we cannot know what the other world is going to be.[95]

Once the wayfarer is launched on the road of life and begins its odyssey, there is no turning back or end. The final destination is spiritual nearness to God and acquisition of His attributes and perfections, a continuous process, since they are endless. This is the destiny of every soul, even those that have separated themselves from God. The holy books call these souls 'dead'; that is, although they continue to exist, they do not enjoy real spiritual 'life'.

What of those souls that have turned away from God in the second stage of their odyssey? Are they in the same position as those who have turned towards God? The Bahá'í teachings explain:

> This . . . does not mean that the souls separated from God are equal, whether they perform good or bad actions. It signifies only that the foundation is to know God, and the good actions result from this knowledge. Nevertheless, it is certain that between the good, the sinners and the wicked who are veiled from God there is a difference. For the veiled one who has good principles and character deserves the pardon of God, while he who is a sinner, and has bad qualities and character, is deprived of the bounties and blessings of God.[96]

> Let no one imagine that by Our assertion that all created things are the signs of the revelation of God is meant that – God forbid – all men, be they good or evil, pious or infidel, are equal in the sight of God.[97]

What happens to those souls who on earth do not have the opportunity to recognize and accept the Manifestation of God for the epoch, and therefore do not fulfil the high destiny ordained for them? Shoghi Effendi explains:

Those who have never had any opportunity of hearing of the Faith but who lived good lives will no doubt be treated with the greatest love and mercy in the next world and reap their full reward.[98]

And:

Concerning your question whether a soul can receive knowledge of the Truth in the world beyond. Such a knowledge is surely possible, and is but a sign of the loving Mercy of the Almighty. We can, through our prayers, help every soul to gradually attain this high station, even if it has failed to reach it in this world. The progress of the soul does not come to an end with death. It rather starts along a new line. Bahá'u'lláh teaches that great far-reaching possibilities await the soul in the other world. Spiritual progress in that realm is infinite, and no man, while on this earth, can visualize its full power and extent.[99]

Some may wonder what is the destiny of the souls who leave the first and second stages of their odyssey as babies or young children. The Bahá'í teachings assure us that special bounties and protection await them:

These infants are under the shadow of the favour of God; and as they have not committed any sin and are not soiled with the impurities of the world of nature, they are the centres of the manifestation of bounty, and the Eye of Compassion will be turned upon them.[100]

Indeed, 'Abdu'l-Bahá, in consoling the parents of a child who had died, makes it clear that any soul leaving the second stage of its odyssey for the third is blessed:

The inscrutable divine wisdom underlieth such heart-rending occurrences. It is as if a kind gardener transferreth a fresh and tender shrub from a confined place to a wide open area. This transfer is not the cause of the withering, the lessening or the destruction of that shrub; nay, on the contrary, it maketh it to grow and thrive, acquire freshness and delicacy, become green and bear fruit. This hidden secret is well known to the gardener, but those souls who are unaware of this bounty suppose that the gardener, in his anger and wrath, hath uprooted the shrub. Yet to those who are aware, this concealed fact is manifest, and this predestined decree is considered a bounty. Do not feel grieved or disconsolate, therefore, at the ascension of that bird of faithfulness; nay, under all circumstances pray for that youth, supplicating for him forgiveness and the elevation of his station.[101]

How many celestial worlds the wayfarer is going to traverse and what wonderful spiritual experiences is he going to have if he always seeks the protection and guidance of his Creator. In the words of Bahá'u'lláh:

O My servants! Sorrow not if, in these days and on this earthly plane, things contrary to your wishes have been ordained and manifested by God, for days of blissful joy, of heavenly delight, are assuredly in store for you. Worlds, holy and spiritually glorious, will be unveiled to your eyes. You are destined by Him, in this world and hereafter, to partake of their benefits, to share in their joys, and to obtain a portion of their sustaining grace. To each and every one of them you will, no doubt, attain.[102]

For every one of you his paramount duty is to choose for himself that on which no other may infringe and none usurp from him. Such a thing – and to this the Almighty is My witness – is the love of God, could ye but perceive it.

Build ye for yourselves such houses as the rain and floods can never destroy, which shall protect you from the changes and chances of this life. This is the instruction of Him Whom the world hath wronged and forsaken.[103]

Epilogue

The Supreme Goal

ALTHOUGH THIS SUMMARY of the odyssey of the soul may appear to some to be a work of fiction, it is reality itself – the road mapped out for us by the Creator, as revealed by His divine Manifestation. It is impossible to over-estimate the importance of our actions and conduct in this world in relation to our future life in the Kingdom. When we consider that our journey, after leaving this world, is for all eternity, it behoves us to meditate deeply on it. As Shoghi Effendi warns:

> Every other Word of Bahá'u'lláh's and 'Abdu'l-Bahá's Writings is a preachment on moral and ethical conduct; all else is the form, the chalice, into which the pure spirit must be poured; without the spirit and the action which must demonstrate it, it is a lifeless form.
>
> [For example] Bahá'u'lláh says adultery retards the progress of the soul in the after life – so grievous is it . . .[104]

The only purpose of the entire creation is that the human being know the Creator and attain His presence. The only way to fulfil this supreme goal is to recognize and accept the Manifestation of God for the epoch in which one lives – today, Bahá'u'lláh – and to observe sincerely His teachings and laws.

Everything else is of secondary importance. The following words of Bahá'u'lláh merit sincere and unbiased reflection:

> . . . every man hath been, and will continue to be, able of himself to appreciate the Beauty of God, the Glorified. Had he not been endowed with such a capacity, how could he be called to account for his failure? If, in the Day when all the peoples of the earth will be gathered together, any man should, whilst standing in the presence of God, be asked: 'Wherefore hast thou disbelieved in My Beauty and turned away from My Self,' and if such a man should reply and say: 'Inasmuch as all men have erred, and none hath been found willing to turn his face to the Truth, I, too, following their example, have grievously failed to recognize the Beauty of the Eternal,' such a plea will, assuredly, be rejected. For the faith of no man can be conditioned by any one except himself.[105]

> The first duty prescribed by God for His servants is the recognition of Him Who is the Day Spring of His Revelation and the Fountain of His laws, Who representeth the Godhead in both the Kingdom of His Cause and the world of creation. Whoso achieveth this duty hath attained unto all good; and whoso is deprived thereof, hath gone astray, though he be the author of every righteous deed. It behoveth every one who reacheth this most sublime station, this summit of transcendent glory, to observe every ordinance of Him Who is the Desire of the world. These twin duties are inseparable. Neither is acceptable without the other. Thus hath it been decreed by Him Who is the Source of Divine inspiration.[106]

All that our Creator desires and has ordained for us is our welfare, progress and eternal happiness. As Bahá'u'lláh states:

O My servants! Could ye apprehend with what wonders of My munificence and bounty I have willed to entrust your souls, ye would, of a truth, rid yourselves of attachment to all created things, and would gain a true knowledge of your own selves – a knowledge which is the same as the comprehension of Mine own Being. Ye would find yourselves independent of all else but Me, and would perceive, with your inner and outer eye, and as manifest as the revelation of My effulgent Name, the seas of My loving-kindness and bounty moving within you.[107]

And 'Abdu'l-Bahá confirms:

Know thou that the Kingdom is the real world, and this nether place is only its shadow stretching out. A shadow hath no life of its own; its existence is only a fantasy, and nothing more; it is but images reflected in water, and seeming as pictures to the eye.[108]

Divine Justice

A NUMBER, perhaps a large number, of people around the world do not believe in God, or have doubts about His existence. They look to the injustices of the world, to the oppression of the innocent, to the excessive opulence and power of an elite and the abject material poverty of the majority, to the rigid discrimination against certain sections of the population, and so on. Such people say that if God existed, He would not permit all this. It is a subject that troubles many sincere and thoughtful people and which needs much deep and detached reflection.

The following observations may help. First, these conditions do exist and even prevail, but they are not the fault of God but rather of the inhabitants of the earth. God has always sent His divine Manifestations to the world to educate and guide us along the right road. If we do not accept and follow their wise counsels and good example, the blame is ours, not our Creator's. He has conferred on us the faculty of free will – the power to choose between good and evil, right and wrong, this road and that. If we choose wrongly or unwisely, the whole of humanity has to suffer the consequences, for humanity is a single organism.

Second, Bahá'u'lláh has been sent by our Creator at this time with the sacred mission of establishing a new world order, divine in origin, unique in character, glorious in purpose, and based on divine teachings and laws – the long awaited Kingdom of God promised by Christ and the other Prophets and Messengers. When this new order is established, while the world will still be a 'first classroom', the great majority of the present abuses and injustices will gradually pass away.

Third, in any event – and this is the crux of the matter – in reality a perfect and complete justice does exist but we are unable to perceive it unless we understand and view life from a spiritual standpoint and see it in its total extension through all the worlds of God.

Every person is a spiritual being whose real home is the spiritual world and not this fleeting, ephemeral world. Life on earth is a matter of only a few years, while the soul's existence is for all eternity. God has always declared, through His Manifestations, that it is in the world, or worlds, beyond that the soul will receive the majority of its recompense for its good deeds, as well as retribution for its misdeeds. If we really understand and accept this, all gradually falls into place and we perceive complete and perfect justice.

Truly, if God did not exist and life did not continue after the death of our physical body, existence itself would have no meaning or reason for being, nor would all the grief and struggle in this material world be worthwhile. One spends years acquiring knowledge and experience and, hopefully, at least some understanding, wisdom and maturity. If life terminates at that point, all had no purpose, no fruit. Our reason, and something deep down in our innermost being, tell us, if we listen, that there has to be something more. As 'Abdu'l-Bahá so clearly says:

> Consider the aim of creation: is it possible that all is created to evolve and develop through countless ages with this small goal in view – a few years of a man's life on earth? Is it not unthinkable that this should be the final aim of existence? . . .
>
> At the best, man spends four-score years and ten in this world – a short time indeed!
>
> Does a man cease to exist when he leaves the body? If his life comes to an end, then all the previous evolution is useless, all has been for nothing! Can one imagine that Creation has no greater aim than this?
>
> . . . It is only a man without intelligence who, after considering these things, can imagine that the great scheme of creation should suddenly cease to progress, that evolution should come to such an inadequate end![109]

> And if a human life, with its spiritual being, were limited to this earthly span, then what would be the harvest of creation? Indeed, what would be the effects and the outcomes of Divinity Itself? Were such a notion true, then all created things, all contingent realities, and this whole world of being – all would be meaningless. God forbid that one should hold to such a fiction and gross error.[110]

HEAR ME, ye mortal birds! In the Rose Garden of changeless splendour a Flower hath begun to bloom, compared to which every other flower is but a thorn, and before the brightness of Whose glory the very essence of beauty must pale and wither. Arise, therefore, and, with the whole enthusiasm of your hearts, with all the eagerness of your souls, the full fervour of your will, and the concentrated efforts of your entire being, strive to attain the paradise of His presence, and endeavour to inhale the fragrance of the incorruptible Flower, to breathe the sweet savours of holiness, and to obtain a portion of this perfume of celestial glory. Whoso followeth this counsel will break his chains asunder, will taste the abandonment of enraptured love, will attain unto his heart's desire, and will surrender his soul into the hands of his Beloved. Bursting through his cage, he will, even as the bird of the spirit, wing his flight to his holy and everlasting nest.[111]

Bibliography

Bibliography

'Abdu'l-Bahá. *Paris Talks*. London: Bahá'í Publishing
    Trust, 1979.
— *The Promulgation of Universal Peace*. Compiled by
    Howard MacNutt. Wilmette, Illinois: Bahá'í
    Publishing Trust, 1982.
— *Selections from the Writings of 'Abdu'l-Bahá*.
    Compiled by the Research Department of the
    Universal House of Justice. Translated by a Comittee
    at the Bahá'í World Centre and Marzieh Gail. Haifa:
    Bahá'í World Centre, 1978.
— *Some Answered Questions*. Collected and translated
    from the Persian by Laura Clifford Barney. Wilmette,
    Illinois: Bahá'í Publishing Trust, 1990.
The Báb, *Selections from the Writings of the Báb*.
    Compiled by the Research Department of the
    Universal House of Justice and translated by Habib
    Taherzadeh with the assistance of a Committee at the
    Bahá'í World Centre. Haifa: Bahá'í World Centre,
    1976.
Bahá'í World Faith. Selected Writings of Bahá'u'lláh and
    'Abdu'l-Bahá. Wilmette, Illinois: Bahá'í Publishing
    Trust, 1971.
Bahá'u'lláh. *Gleanings from the Writings of Bahá'u'lláh*.
    Compiled and translated by Shoghi Effendi.
    Wilmette, Illinois: Bahá'í Publishing Trust, 2nd rev.
    edn. 1984.

— *The Hidden Words*. Translated by Shoghi Effendi with the assistance of some English friends. Wilmette, Illinois: Bahá'í Publishing Trust, 1990.

— *Kitáb-i-Íqán*. Translated by Shoghi Effendi. Wilmette, Illinois: Bahá'í Publishing Trust, 1989.

— *The Seven Valleys and The Four Valleys*. Translated by Marzieh Gail, in consultation with Ali Kuli Khan. Wilmette, Illinois: Bahá'í Publishing Trust, 1991.

— *Tablets of Bahá'u'lláh revealed after the Kitáb-i-Aqdas*. Compiled by the Research Department of the Universal House of Justice and translated by Habib Taherzadeh with the assistance of a Committee at the Bahá'í World Centre. Wilmette, Illinois: Bahá'í Publishing Trust, 1988.

The Compilation of Compilations. Prepared by the Universal House of Justice 1963–1990. 2 vols. Sydney: Bahá'í Publications Australia, 1991.

Directives from the Guardian. Compiled by Gertrude Garrida. New Delhi: Bahá'í Publishing Trust, 1973.

The Divine Art of Living. Compiled by Mabel Hyde Paine and revised by Anne Marie Scheffer. Wilmette, Illinois: Bahá'í Publishing Trust, rev. edn. 1986.

Esslemont, J. E. *Bahá'u'lláh and the New Era*. London: Bahá'í Publishing Trust, 1974.

Lights of Guidance. Compiled by Helen Hornby. New Delhi: Bahá'í Publishing Trust, rev. edn. 1988.

Shoghi Effendi. *The Advent of Divine Justice*. Wilmette, Illinois: Bahá'í Publishing Trust, 1990.

— *God Passes By*. Wilmette, Illinois: Bahá'í Publishing Trust, 1970.

— *The Promised Day is Come*. Wilmette, Illinois: Bahá'í Publishing Trust, rev. edn. 1980.

Star of the West. Rpt. in 8 vols. Oxford: George Ronald, 1978.

References

References

1. Bahá'u'lláh, *Hidden Words*, Arabic 14.
2. 'Abdu'l-Bahá, *Paris Talks*, p. 85.
3. ibid. p. 91.
4. Bahá'u'lláh, *Gleanings*, LXXX, p. 155.
5. ibid. CI, p. 206.
6. ibid. CXXXII, p. 287.
7. ibid. CXII, pp. 259–60.
8. Bahá'u'lláh, *Hidden Words*, Arabic 21.
9. ibid. Arabic 22.
10. ibid. Arabic 23.
11. Bahá'u'lláh, *Gleanings*, XXIX, p. 70.
12. ibid. CXLVIII, pp. 317–18.
13. ibid. XIX, pp. 46–7. The nature of the Creator is explained in a letter written on behalf of Shoghi Effendi:

    What is meant by a personal God is a God Who is conscious of His creation, Who has a Mind, a Will, a Purpose, and not, as many scientists and materialists believe, an unconscious and determined force operating in the universe. Such conception of the Divine Being, as the Supreme and ever present Reality in the world, is not anthropomorphic, for it transcends all human limitations and forms, and does by no means attempt to define the essence of Divinity which is obvi-

ously beyond any human comprehension. To say
that God is a personal Reality does not mean that
He has a physical form, or does in any way resemble
a human being. To entertain such belief would
be sheer blasphemy. (From a letter written on
behalf of Shoghi Effendi to an individual believer,
21 April 1939, cited in *Lights*, no. 1574, p. 477.)

14. ibid. XXI, pp. 49–50.
15. ibid. p. 50.
16. ibid. XXVII, pp. 65.
17. ibid. pp. 65–6.
18. See, for example, 'Abdu'l-Bahá, *Promulgation*,
    p. 258 and *Some Answered Questions*, pp. 208–9.
19. Shoghi Effendi, *God Passes By*, p. 94.
20. Bahá'u'lláh, *Gleanings*, X, pp. 12–13. Bahá'u'lláh
    spent the last 24 years of His life in the Holy Land.
    Here He revealed the Kitáb-i-Aqdas, the new laws of
    God for humanity. The World Centre of the Bahá'í
    Faith is now established there on Mount Carmel,
    Haifa.
21. 'Abdu'l-Bahá, *Some Answered Questions*, p. 279.
22. Bahá'u'lláh, *Kitáb-i-Íqán*, p. 120.
23. ibid. pp. 254–5.
24. Bahá'u'lláh, *Gleanings*, CLIII, pp. 328–9.
25. ibid. CXXVIII, p. 276.
26. Bahá'u'lláh, *Tablets*, p. 24.
27. ibid. p. 71.
28. ibid. p. 26.
29. Bahá'u'lláh, *Gleanings*, LXXI, p. 138.
30. 'Abdu'l-Bahá, *Paris Talks*, p. 178.
31. From a letter dated 22 November 1936 written on
    behalf of Shoghi Effendi to an individual believer.

Cited in *Compilation*, vol. 2, no. 1281, p. 7.

32. From a letter dated 5 November 1931 written on behalf of Shoghi Effendi to an individual believer. Cited in *Compilation*, vol. 2, no. 1274, p. 4.

33. From a letter dated 5 August 1949 written on behalf of Shoghi Effendi to an individual believer. Cited in *Compilation*, vol. 2, no. 1322, p. 20.

34. 'Abdu'l-Bahá, *Paris Talks*, pp. 50–1.

35. ibid. p. 179.

36. 'Abdu'l-Bahá, in *Divine Art of Living*, p. 87.

37. Bahá'u'lláh, *Hidden Words*, Arabic 51.

38. Bahá'u'lláh, *Kitáb-i-Íqán*, p. 39.

39. Bahá'u'lláh, *Hidden Words*, Arabic 5.

40. 'Abdu'l-Bahá, *Promulgation*, pp. 148–9.

41. 'Abdu'l-Bahá, from a Tablet to an American Bahá'í, translated by Ali Kuli Khan, October 1908, cited in Esslemont, *New Era*, p. 89.

42. Attributed to 'Abdu'l-Bahá.

43. 'Abdu'l-Bahá, cited in *Pattern of Bahá'í Life*, p. 55.

44. The Báb, *Selections*, p. 78.

45. Bahá'u'lláh, *Gleanings*, CXXXVI, p. 295.

46. Bahá'u'lláh, *Kitáb-i-Íqán*, p. 238.

47. 'Abdu'l-Bahá, *Bahá'í World Faith*, p. 383.

48. From a letter written on behalf of Shoghi Effendi to an individual believer, 19 November 1945. Cited in *Lights of Guidance*, no. 1484, p. 456.

49. 'Abdu'l-Bahá, *Paris Talks*, p. 174.

50. ibid. p. 175.

51. ibid.

52. ibid.

53. ibid.

54. ibid. p. 176.

55. Bahá'u'lláh, *Hidden Words*, Arabic 2.

56. Bahá'u'lláh, *Kitáb-i-Íqán*, pp. 195–7.

57. 'Abdu'l-Bahá, cited in Shoghi Effendi, *Promised Day is Come*, p. 119.

58. Shoghi Effendi, *Advent,* p. 16.

59. 'Abdu'l-Bahá, cited in *Divine Art of Living*, p. 61.

60. 'Abdu'l-Bahá, *Some Answered Questions*, p. 237.

61. Bahá'u'lláh, *Gleanings*, CXIII, p. 226.

62. ibid. LXXXVI, p. 171.

63. ibid. CXIV, p. 236.

64. Bahá'u'lláh, *Hidden Words*, Arabic 31.

65. Bahá'u'lláh. *Gleanings*, LII, p. 106.

66. 'Abdu'l-Bahá, *Promulgation*, p. 217.

67. Bahá'u'lláh, *Gleanings*, V, p. 8.

68. Talk of 'Abdu'l-Bahá given in Stuttgart, copy in possession of the author.

69. 'Abdu'l-Bahá, *Selections*, pp. 193–5.

70. Bahá'u'lláh, *Gleanings*, LXXXI, pp. 156–7.

71. ibid. p. 157.

72. 'Abdu'l-Bahá, in *Divine Art of Living*, pp. 37–8.

73. 'Abdu'l-Bahá, *Some Answered Questions*, p. 241.

74. Bahá'u'lláh, *Gleanings*, LXXXI, p. 157.

75. 'Abdu'l-Bahá, *Selections*, p. 194.

76. 'Abdu'l-Bahá, cited in Esslemont, *New Era*, p. 175.

77. From a letter written on behalf of the Guardian to the National Spiritual Assembly of India, 10 March 1936. *Lights of Guidance*, no. 694, p. 207.

78. Bahá'u'lláh, *Gleanings*, LXXXI, p. 156.

79. ibid. LXXXVI, pp. 169–70.

80. 'Abdu'l-Bahá, *Some Answered Questions*, p. 240.

81. ibid. p. 231.

82. 'Abdu'l-Bahá, cited in Esslemont, *New Era*, p. 178.

83. From a letter written on behalf of Shoghi Effendi to an individual believer, 10 December 1952. *Lights of Guidance*, no. 679, p. 204.

84. 'Abdu'l-Bahá, *Some Answered Questions*, p. 231.

85. 'Abdu'l-Bahá, cited in Esslemont, *New Era*, p. 175.

86. 'Abdu'l-Bahá, *Selections*, p. 193.

87. 'Abdu'l-Bahá, cited in Esslemont, *New Era*, pp. 178–9.

88. 'Abdu'l-Bahá, cited in ibid. p. 178.

89. From a letter written on behalf of the Guardian to an individual believer, 4 March 1946. *Lights of Guidance*, no. 1735, p. 513.

90. Bahá'u'lláh, *Seven Valleys*, pp. 32–3.

91. 'Abdu'l-Bahá, *Some Answered Questions*, p. 228.

92. Bahá'u'lláh, *Gleanings*, LXXIX, pp. 152–3.

93. ibid. pp. 151–2.

94. ibid. LXXXI, pp. 155–6.

95. From a letter written on behalf of the Guardian to an individual believer, 18 October 1932. *Lights of Guidance*. no. 682, p. 204.

96. 'Abdu'l-Bahá, *Some Answered Questions*, p. 238.

97. Bahá'u'lláh, *Gleanings*, XCIII, p. 187.

98. Shoghi Effendi, *Directives of the Guardian*, p. 39.

99. From a letter written on behalf of the Guardian to an

individual believer, 22 May 1935. *Lights of Guidance*, no. 683, p. 204.

100. 'Abdu'l-Bahá, *Some Answered Questions*, p. 240.

101. 'Abdu'l-Bahá, *Selections*, pp. 199–200.

102. Bahá'u'lláh, *Gleanings*, CLIII, p. 329.

103. ibid. CXXIII, p. 261.

104. From letter written on behalf of the Guardian to an individual believer, 30 September 1949. *Lights of Guidance*, no. 1159, p. 345.

105. Bahá'u'lláh, *Gleanings*, LXXV, p. 143.

106. ibid. CLV, pp. 330–1.

107. ibid. CLIII, pp. 326–7.

108. 'Abdu'l-Bahá, *Selections*, p. 178.

109. 'Abdu'l-Bahá, *Paris Talks*, pp. 92–4.

110. 'Abdu'l-Bahá, *Selections*, p. 185.

111. Bahá'u'lláh, *Gleanings*, CLI, pp. 320–1.